Will Work

for Food

A Book of Inspiration,

Poems, and Edible Action

by jared posey

a SACRED ❖ TASK book

To Kim Heacox, who taught me not how to be a writer, but that I am one.

And to Katie, my wife, and to our child in her womb. Everything I write is for you.

Contents

-Appendix-

A Note to the Reader

If you're new to poetry, thanks for visiting. If I may suggest, read aloud slowly (or at least mouth the words a little bit). Sound is everything. If you read each poem more than once, you'll definitely tap into more meaning. Most important of all, have fun. It's not a competition and it's not a test. It's sheet music. It's a playground for spirit.

Poetry is a lot like meditation—it works better if you relax. Don't demand or expect concrete meanings. A poem is a feeling. It's a moment. It's this moment. And superior to its medium is its message. This is about our present and our future, not my hobby.

These words are dedicated to the capacity of each person holding this book. The revolution will not be televised. It will be within.

-jp

"There is, then, a politics of food that, like any politics, involves our freedom. We still (sometimes) remember that we cannot be free if our minds and voices are controlled by someone else. But we have neglected to understand that we cannot be free if our food and its sources are controlled by someone else. The condition of the passive consumer of food is not a democratic condition. One reason to eat responsibly is to live free."

-Wendell Berry

Will Work For Food

You're right, we cannot change
The World. And we cannot rewrite
The History. And Human Nature
is no blank slate. And try as we may,
you and I don't add up
to The Government. And I can't
and won't house Our Destiny,
won't carry Our Fate.
And we couldn't change
The Past or The Future
if we tried. However,

it will work for food.
We _can_ change that.
So, stop telling me we can't and start
helping me do it.

Dollar Create/shun Dance

Dollar dollar

  Farm next door

Dollar dollar

  Grocery store

Dollar dollar

  Superstore

Dollar dollar

  More and more

Dollar dollar

  Decisions which we make with it affect
our health future children sanity society
sense of humor, and laundromat, we can
create and destroy, we can build ecologies
and starve empires, we are the masters of
our own economy, let's stop talking like
we're powerless simply because the
impossible doesn't seem so possible yet,

2

let's start making something of something
and stop supporting what we don't
believe in, after all what is the world but
our world, and what is our world but the
world, the sum is the parts and all that
and greater, so if we change nothing we
change nothing, after all what are
opposable thumbs good for if they only
push buttons, green thumbs push buttons
too, I believe that the soil is real and that
I've used too many commas, but why use
periods in a continuum, and why stop
living while alive, and that maybe we can
liberate ourselves by liberating ourselves,
through our actions regardless of all that
other doubletalk doubletalk, I mean what
do you want to do, give or give up?

Bedtime Stories

I'm like you.

I try to do things.

I carry around the results

counting the money

in my head,

telling myself stories

and believing them.

I tally my life

into wins and losses.

And, like you, I too

at times have those moments

with my knees

on the ground

and my fingers

burying into the black

crust of soil

and my lips just smiling

a thousand riches,

or disobeying the rules

at one o'clock writing away

sleep into poems,

unable to stop the commas,

unwilling to halt

the madness of being

—but really the details

don't matter—

cause I too have found

what matters.

I too have carried

its meaning.

For Albert Camus

We cannot perfect

the world. But we do

affect it.

Perhaps it is not possible

to live in a world

of no ecological harm.

But we can lessen its frequency.

We can diminish its presence.

And we should.

(Expertise)-ism

A food scientist <u>knows</u> the sensory analysis
        of the foods I eat,
<u>knows</u> the molecular composition
        of an apple.

Food engineers (can) dictate enzymes and
    usher in the conversion of specific acids
    and sugars,
(can) reconstitute the energy of life,
(can) manipulate molecules and isolate
    genes,
(can) map the ratios of micronutrients, and
(can) modify how foods will interact with
    my neurochemistry, my endocrine
    system, my gastrointestinal tract.

In fact, food experts <u>know</u> my body

better than I do.

They <u>know</u> the physiochemical principles

   underlying food preservation and

(can) boost shelf-life to years,

(can) make thickening agents, sweeteners,

   flavor enhancers, texture enhancers,

   coloring agents

            out of corn on the cob,

(can) provide definitions for emollient,

   polysaccharide, rheological, eicosanoid,

   linoleic, carboxylic

            out of English,

(can) transform the alphabet into long,

   polymeric chains of chemical symbols,

(can) change how I smell something, how I

   taste something, how I see something,

   what I feel.

You see, food scientists <u>can</u> engineer *perfect*
food.

But do they (know) enough not to?

And do they (know)
who the expert is?

All foods not created =

1. animals equal nothing
more than lbs units and packages.
Wrapped neatly in plastic,
they come in red or black. They're
either on sale or they're not.

2. plants are *just*-plants.
They should be un-bruised
and un-lumpy. They should always
look the same. Unimportant
where they come from,
plants are just-plants.
They better be cheap and clean.

Three. On the farm
with chickens. The mood was quiet
but not regretful. We took them

one at a time, as individuals,

and held them by their feet

upside down until their biology

went still. We slid their head through

a cone, their body hugged

by cold plastic.

I took a sharp blade

and pushed aside the feathers on

its neck. The metal felt raw and hot

as I steadied it over the creature's flesh.

I don't know if the bird was looking

at me or if that was just me

looking at myself. I pressed the knife

quickly and deeply. The blood

spilled over my fingers and into the earth.

The bird's body shook violently

in spasms as it bled out, its nervous

system slowly accepting fate.

It was dark.

There was nothing clean
about it, yet nothing
not sacred.

small is Beautiful

Imagine the government waking up
tomorrow with a change of heart
and deciding to clean up their politics...

in an instant dramatically reducing
corruption, partisan bickering, and
bureaucratic inefficiency. The day after
tomorrow, things are incredibly better.

You might respond that I'm gullible
to sophomoric daydreams.
And I might ask why those with power
don't cash it in for meaning.

It is only from distant glances
that has us thinking that evolution acts on
the level of species.

Rather, it is varying groups of individuals

that act
and are acted upon. individuals.
Bottom-up adaptation.

Imagine me deciding now
and choosing, in this instant, that I will eat
better, speak kinder, and live my life
with an unspeakable gratitude.

Why shouldn't I?
…In fact, I shall.
I'm small enough to do so.

You can tell me it won't change anything.
But in the time you said that,
I already have.

At the Temple

Healthcare begins with care for our health
and THE ECONOMY begins with ecology.
People talk about THE ECONOMY as if it is
some fearsome god and we must do its
bidding. The economy is not magical. It is
not supernatural. It is an abstraction of *us*.
And if we can change ourselves,

we can change it.

Perfect Food Iz Bad For You

I don't trust no people without blemishes.
Supermarket strawberrys scare me.
Food from the other side of the wurld
simply ain't romantic for me

no more.

i want knobby crooked carrots
covered in dirt from the farmer
down the road. I want to talk to him
or her about earthworms, Wendell Berry
and how we're going

To change the world

For My Niece Avery (someday)

I know you don't yet have *philosophy*.
I know it will be many years before we try
to crack open human nature
together, before we try to figure it all
out, and perhaps feel for a second
as though we have. You haven't yet
experienced your *right* of passage, the
becoming of yourself. I will not lie to you.
The initiation into the world doesn't come
without trauma, without interrupting
the parade of euphemisms, without
breaking clean glass. The truth is, I can't
protect you from the complexity
of life. Wouldn't want to. Imperfection
and impermanence will touch all things.
Just remember, someday,

that it's all okay. Because you can heal

trauma. You can change

the world. And know that your uncle

will be working toward that change, for you

as much as anything, until you're ready

for your time.

Compost   -the Republic-

You are not a food consumer.

You are The Maker

    of movements…

    a Food Citizen deciding

    on Land Use, Domestic Policy

    and Health Care.

You are the Zeus of the grocery

    store, the Beethoven

    of the backyard. You Farm

    the farmers' market.

You are agriculture's

    Agriculture. You can starve empires

and build clay castles. For You

are a Share Holder in Futures.

So don't break down

without a Blessing.

Just a girl

A young girl thumbs the packages

of perfected cornucopias, grazing

on the synthetic rainbows of the grocery

store. As far as she's been

shown, coming here is synonymous

with not dying. She lifts

a couple of food products. She steps over

to a conveyor belt and a uniform to trade

paper for calories. She lifts a magazine,

thumbs its pages as she waits. It is of

women that don't look like her

mother or friends. She doesn't have

the weaponry to articulate that. She pays

and walks back out into the concrete

of her world, still dangerously seeking

sustenance.

?uestion Mark at the End

We need to do this to the land

to feed the world .

Modifying Organisms

GMOs roll the dice on our genetic diversity and oftentimes contribute to significantly larger doses of pesticides. More than anything, they often seem unnecessary, especially when the earth and sun are such willing participants to provide—if we respect and understand their blueprint.

You hear experts say we need to feed the world. Then what happens? They plow up miles of supercorn and supersoy that you and I couldn't or wouldn't—or at the very least—shouldn't eat. Then they synthesize

pseudo food and pseudo drink. Humanity

is a guinea pig, they think, so they fatten up

animals of questionable content at pathetic

pound ratios of feed to meat. Pathetic ratios

of burdens to blessings, economics to ethics.

What is our goal?

Calories or ancestry?

Continuance or cancer?

We're seeing diabetes now in elementary

schools. We're seeing antibiotic resistance

with no alternative for the time we may actually need them. Cows in cages and on crammed lots. Superfoods with more toxins in them than nutrients. Fresh produce crossing oceans. Organic material as toxic waste. Now, we're running out of clean soil clean water clean air. We're running out of new normals. But, mostly, we're running out of creativity, responsibility, and willpower.

And to not modify this—to not modify *us*—would be lame.

On Cultivating

Are books enough?

Are words enough?

Is action itself

even sufficient?

I don't know,

but I know

doing nothing

is not enough,

because we both know

doing nothing

is impossible.

More Like Talking

First, the fact that we even have to bend and talk about economics as a primary factor in matters vital to our health and environment shows how sadly off-course we are. The seven-generation principle reminds us that when we make decisions, we should consider seven generations back, our ancestors, and seven generations forward, our descendants. The present generation cannot step out of its own context—its past and future.

This places our economies, something we in
fact created and thus can change to our
needs and liking, in an appropriate light.
The more that small farmers cultivate food
ethically—with ethics being as much as
anything what they farm—and the more
local citizens support them, the more the
economy in that area benefits its
community. The more those trades actually
belong to and remain in that community.
The more it fosters a culture. The more the
economy belongs to and acts like people.

The system we have is not working.
Industrial food replaces men and women

with technology, miracle, and machine.

Processed food becomes our healthcare

crisis. Our crises. Our diabetes. Our heart's

disease. Pesticides fungicides herbicides

become our cancer. Our family's cancer. The

mutation of our lives. The inhumane

enslavement of animals in tightly-packed,

grassless, windowless enclosures parallels

the disconnect we have from ourselves and

each other. We put ourselves in prisons.

These cells reflect our own diminished

environments and diminished empathies.

Clean soil clean water clean air is the

forgotten foundation of any economy.

Forget it for long and The Creation becomes

Hell. Let economy trump ecology and our

life will tell the story of a slow death. But,

don't worry, we're just talking here.

Out in the Dark (sustenance)

I look up at the moon.

It is deeply still.

I ask it if I can store

my drama there, my worried

thoughts and fears.

It is silent.

It says nothing to me.

It's just what I need.

Bhagavad Eata

I do silly things,

like drinking the pickle juice,

or waterfalling the last crumbs

into my mouth. My wife and I

reinstated plate-licking as acceptable,

partly to not waste those savory last

flavors and nutrients, and partly

because it makes us smile

and feel more like dogs. And I know

an ancient Greek philosopher who said

we should live more like dogs. Then

again, I guess he slept in a bathtub.

Then again, maybe

so should I.

I go to some ridiculous efforts to reuse.

Devoting an hour to washing the peanut

butter out of the jar. Carrying around

orange peels and apple cores

for hours or days until I can

bring them home to compost.

Religiously turning lights off.

I plan to take bucket showers all summer.

No, I don't think I'm the Mother Theresa

of the living room. I'm not the Nelson

Mandela of the garden.

Truthfully, I probably doubt the notion

that I'm making a sizeable difference

with these behaviors. I know how big the

world is. I know how small are the soles

of my feet. But its not my job

to go through life weighing

everything until I become

a weight myself.

I don't need to judge. I don't need to

measure.

I believe I have a duty: to tread lightly,

to dance loudly, and to say hello

when in the presence of birds. So, I perform

my duty. And I don't worry about the rest.

Enter Net (A World Wide Web)

The internet was hooked into my house

today. The web. I first catered to my inbox. I

typed a long letter to a friend. I chatted with

my family, ordered some food, and

shopped around for a new job. I did a little

reading and played some games. I then

began searching, clicking from image to

image, video to video, thread to thread.

Each connected. Each casting me further in.

It was then I began watching videos of

music.

Rap music in America.

The mono-typical.

Self = strength. A slippery soap box.

Standing atop the shoulders of women and

bragging of height. Strength in loneliness.

Lonely strength. Women giving birth. Sexy

models posturing like in consumer ads.

Bending at the knees and childbearing hips.

The look of wanting sex on their faces

strangely believable. Men tugging on chains

and guns as if bragging of metal. As if

aiming at the feminine. Hidden lines drawn

for enemies. Where my ego ends and you

begin. No prophet but profit. Make it 'till

you fake it. One nation under Green. Red

bandanas hang from pants, as if pockets

spill with blood. One shade in blood.

Reminds me of politics. I looked up the

news.

Political news in America.

The stereo-typical.

Red and blue like emergency vehicle sirens.

Like gang paint. Like teenage poetry. He

said she said. Us and them. Black and blue.

Fingerpointing naysaying nothingmongering. A couple of straw man fallacies. Some subliminal namecalling. A vacuum where there was a village. Common ground in a booby-trapped hole. Like war just with language. Like language justified with war. Civilization, getting off on its own connection. Blowing secondhand smoke, contact highs for people of clocks and no time. Two colors. Black and white. Ones and zero.

So, I hibernated the computer. I walked into the kitchen and started nibbling on bits of raw kale, as if clinging to hope, as if trying to say something.

An Apology (Do You Except?)

Listen, Planet, we need to talk.

No, it's not you…

it's me… it's us.

We'd like to apologize, for a lot of things,

but let's start with seedless fruit. I know

we should have just eaten around them, but

it all seemed so fun and innocent at the

time. Like when we started raising animals

in cramped, industrial-style factory farms

and it was so horrible ethically and

environmentally and for our health and all

that. Exactly the same. And listen, the hot

dog. Okay, not our finest hour. But

Germany had those amazing bratwurst

things and we thought we could make that

into something you probably shouldn't eat.

You know, American food.

But, anyways, we're really sorry. Kind of

like how we created a massive dead zone

in the Gulf of Mexico due to runoff from

Midwestern farms being carried down the

Mississippi, or that plastic soup in the

Pacific, a floating garbage garden the size of

Texas, or how we severely overexploited

most fisheries in the world. You know,

same thing. Okay, and maybe we shouldn't have deep-fried Twinkies. But, you have to admit, it was kind of cute. Like the billions of pounds of chemical insecticides and herbicides we use on our *farms* every single year. Also, admit it, slightly adorable.

But, most of all, we're sorry to butter for that whole margarine thing. That should have never happened.

I just want you to know that none of this meant anything to me. Honest, it was just a fling. And yeah, we're still doing all of this, but we can change. You have my word.

Oh, Planet, I know we've cheated on you. I know we're not worthy. Even still, what do you think? Will you take us back? Will you teach us how to love again?

Attention Deficit

These days everything human

begs

for attention

and pleads

for notice.

Twitchy

commercials that

can't

settle

on

an

image. Food labels

that fight wars

of art

and background

battles

on simple verbiage.

Since when does sustenance

need to sell itself?

All-natural!

Cage-free!

Don't these terms

sound a bit

like confessions?

If every resource

is a commodity, if nature is

for sale,

will our lives not become

a transaction, will our consciousness

not become a pop-up ad? Will

"Look at me"

become our epitaph?

But a wild dandelion,

far from any notice,

blossoms silently, with

undeniable necessity, emerges

radiantly from a windblown

seed to a thousand times

its size, without a peep.

It has more nutrition and medicine

than anything you'll find

in a supermarket,

and doesn't need to tell you so.

It has no pricetag.

No ingredients listing.

No artwork other than its head

of flowers. It is proof

of itself. It doesn't ask

to be adored. It demands to be

alive and it is

—attentive—

until the day it accepts its death.

And it doesn't leave the world

with less, but more.

Now, the dandelion didn't ask me

for this, didn't bump into me

with its best reasoning, didn't climb

into my ear with its greatest sales

pitch. It didn't have to.

And that's why

I think I'll give it my

undivided

—gratitude—

That's why I think

I'll give all my attention

to this subtle

surplus.

Don't Have To

All I need is money —

and for that, I must only outsource

my time — and I can have the triple layer

chocolate cake. I can feast

on a 12 oz. sirloin, a pound of shrimp,

a bulk bag of potato chips. I can heat

my house to 80 in the wintertime, make it 60

in the summer — with a button.

I can go outside, start my car,

and leave it running until the gas peters out.

I could

go out and buy unlimited chemical

pesticides, free

of judgment, probably even encouraged

to do so, then spread them all around

my yard. I could set up

a heartless factory farm with the smiling

help of experts. And you might be labeled

unreasonable

if you labeled me unreasonable. After all,

it's my body,

it's my property, it's

my *money*.

But being legal doesn't make something

right. Just because you can, doesn't mean

you should. And just because it's accepted,

doesn't mean it's good.

When intention in living, humility, and

compassion go out of style

—when the truth is no longer popular—

I say stop being popular.

Talk to cows and salamanders if you have

to. Imagine what they need.

Make somebody's day. Sit with a bird.

Hop around like a rabbit. Be nice

to someone. Compliment their hair, their

shoes, their beak.

Get down on your belly and watch

what the dirt does. Watch a sunset upside

down. Then crab walk home. And high-five

that neighbor you don't know very well. Eat

flowers and drink poems. Eat the old

things. Farm the old ways. Think the new

ones. Bake bread. Bare feet.

Admit you're wrong. Make love. Pick fruit.

Play guitar. Own your attitude. Change

your diet. Change your money. Change

your habits. *Change your world.*

After all, just because you don't have to,

doesn't mean you shouldn't.

Teaching Fish to Swim

I can't instruct you

how to save yourself, or ourselves.

I can't tell your branches to grow,

your buds to blossom,

your roots to hold.

I can't teach you to swim

and to float, to decide

and to know.

I can't teach you.

I can't give you what is

already yours.

But you can.

You must.

Supermarket Survivalism

Food processing food packaging food
labeling food like ingredients food variety
corn corn like sugar salt variety food like
sugar bread variety many syllable food food
one syllable food packaging food packaging
food shipped in food packaging like food
like product similar to food sprayed with
not food like product like products not food
food one syllable food like labeling not like
food product

Which makes me wonder: where is the

food?

(It's intention is to confuse. It makes you not

want to read into it.)

"Eating is an agricultural act"

which is an ecological one…

Our eco- is our bio-

Our biology

Our biography

Our story

Airsoilwater

How we eat is how we

live

So what happens if we gas

the air?

What if we taunt

climates?

What happens to our soil

when ecosystems become

monocultures sprayed

with new chemicals?

What happens when the land

pollutes the water

and when we ransack the oceans

and leave trace of metals and plastics?

In many ways these problems—our

problems—are food related, as how we eat

is how we live.

What could be more foundational?

More inescapable?

As in, what could be a greater pivot

for change?

So, here's the good news…

you are implicated

not just in the problem

but in the solution

The shared experience

is the food

The common denominator

is you

Poor People

Man, I just feel awful for that guy. My

neighbor, he has it so bad. His whole

property. Every bit of it. The entire yard is

that way. And every year, he tries and tries,

and it just seems to get worse. I know he's

been to home improvement stores asking all

sorts of advice and trying different

products. But nothing seems to help. Its

pretty bad. He spends so much time out

there, and…nothing. Gosh, I feel for him.

I mean the whole yard, the entire thing, is

covered in this grass that spreads all across

their property. I'm not sure if it's a disease

or what happened. It just takes everything

over. Probably one of those invasives. Man,

those invasives are a raw deal. Taking

everything else out. The other stuff just

can't compete. Everywhere you look, it's

just...green. Just one thing for the whole

thing. That's rough.

And dang, not even dandelions. Missing

out on those yellow blooms of flowers that

would look so nice. I bet his wife just bums

out on that. I see her out there. She has to

plant these flowers in pots and hang them

around the porch. They just don't grow in

the yard anymore. That must drive her

crazy. She must really wish that flowers

would just grow in her yard again, like the

good old days. Some little violets and some

thistles. Some red clover. But, man, those

invasives. They really take hold. And then

it's game over.

I wonder if his kids are having issues

because of it. It probably makes them feel

all insecure, all paranoid about their image.

Kids latch onto that stuff. They take it so

seriously. But how would you feel? Just one

plant dominating their whole yard, looking

all diseased or something. It's unnatural. It's

an abomination. And heck, I just feel bad

for them. I bet they feel so awful. Poor kids.

They don't even have white clover over

there. No watching the bees buzz and land

on their little white flowers. Or counting the

petals and looking for that rare treasure: a

four-leaf clover.

And they miss the time when the dandelion

heads go white and my neighbor would

have this beautiful little symbol that he

could use to explain stuff to his kids—like

how life works, or how galaxies are, or on

finding joy in the simple things. I mean

those flower heads are like looking at

starlight for kids. And then no butterflies.

There's just no butterflies over there

anymore. And it's pretty much just robins

that remain. The rest of the birds just

couldn't watch. I guess they left.

And gosh, he spends so much time on it.

Spraying things all the time. Obviously

desperate. Just wants all the other plants to

come back. But they don't. Just that grass.

That crazy grass. That stuff is tough. Every

week he goes out on this expensive machine

he had to buy and he tries to cut it all down.

But that grass just grows and grows back. I think once or twice a week he's out there hacking away at the stuff.

Then it creates such a mess. It covers the whole yard with what he's trimmed. I see him bagging it all up. What a chore. And then he has to pay for it to be picked up with the garbage. And he still doesn't win. It keeps growing back, just that one thing. And then I see him watering it. Must be trying to flood it out, see if he can kill it. He even sets up these elaborate sprinkler systems. Little death traps. He must be trying to catch it off-guard and really

drench it out of there.

You know, come to think of it, it really must

be one of those invasives, or some sort of

disease or something, because now that I

think of it, his neighbor's yard is doing the

exact same thing. I've been noticing that

more and more, all around the

neighborhood. Everybody sure is struggling

with it.

It's tough luck is what it is. But, I guess

that's the way it goes. That's just how it is.

What can you do? But, ya know, life goes

on. Really the guy has nothing to worry

about. I bet someday people won't even

notice it. Heck, sooner or later, it might even

become normal.

The Paradox of THE WORLD

For breakfast I could do <u>eggs</u>

Scramble,, Easy,, Poach,,

FreeRange,, Local,, Veg-Fed,,

Cage-free,, OmegaAdded,,

Jumbo;

I could do oatmeal

Stovetop,, Baked,,

Sweet,, Savory,,

ThickRolled,, SteelCut,, QuickCook,,

Quaker;

Add honey

WildFlowers,, OrangeBlossoms,,

Raw,, Creamy,, Clover,,

HoneyCooked,, HoneyComb,,

HoneyBear;

Sprinkle on some cinnamon

Bark,, Sticks,, Ground,,

Saigon,, Ceylon,,

NonIrradiated,, NonFumigated,,

Powder;

Throw on berries

Blue,, Black,, Straw,, or Blended,,

Fresh,, Frozen,, or FreezeDried,,

European,, Argentinean,, American,,

Jam;

I could even substitute

quinoa for oats!

(White,, Tri-Colored,, Red,,

Inca Gold;)

I could combine

the two!

or do muesli! or fry up some meat!

Quasi?Organic?

Legitimately?Local?

Fake Meat?Pseudo meat!

I could bookdive

into the health to self of

Wheat,, or Meat,, or Too Much

of This,, That,, and The Other Thing;

Stroll the Store,, or Grow

at home;

I mean really

should I make the absolute

best choice about this,, or be all cool

detached enlightened about it?

Which brings me back to this

whole world thing—

there's a thin line between

freedom and a breaking point;

between opportunity and collapse;

there's a consequence to such

choices,,

But, anyways, I guess I'll just have…

<u>lunch</u>.

Smells Fishy

You ever wonder about the language?

Words carry images,

but they can also carry

lies, and sometimes

they just don't seem right.

75 miles of fishing line

from a ship the size

of a football field,

baited with hundreds

of thousands

of hooks

is "fishing"?

Even "commercial fishing"

sounds relatively innocent.

"Industrial fishing"

might be getting closer.

But including the word

"fishing"? What we grow up

doing with our dads?

I don't know. Seems

a confusion of terms.

Somebody messed up...

or plotted something.

Like dragging along

the seafloor at 6,000 feet

with 60,000 pound nets

full of weights and doors

and chains, and metal wheels

pulling these massive nets

and scraping along the floor

of the ocean, making

coral reef clearcuts,

where 90%

of the total catch

is bycatch, that is, unintended,

that is, now dead, other species.

Wait…fishing?

You're going to put that

under the umbrella

of fishing?

Or, bottom trawling?

Isn't that intentionally vague?

I'm trying to think

what would suffice.

Extraction? Mining?

Warfare? Murder?

I don't know.

But, I'll tell you one thing,

if that's fishing,

then I'm the Buddha.

Looking Glass, Houses and Stones

The world seems fully prepped

for cynicism. All ready to go. How could

you resist the thousands of years in the

making, the taking ourselves so seriously?

How we kill by the millions over ideas and

wear shoes and write constitutions and

separate ourselves so cleanly from nature.

How we have baby formulas and quadratic

equations.

How could you resist the species that

brought you the atom bomb, the Adam's

apple, or the Addams Family? All our

games of make-believe. Printing up paper

and calling it more valuable than the trees it

came from. Marching our militaries, as if

war is something neat, orderly, and

impressive.

Have you turned on a television?

Have you cracked open a newspaper?

Have you seen us crap in porcelain thrones?

Here's some news for you: we're easy

to ridicule.

In fact, I often wonder if this whole society is a self-satire, and everyone's in on it, that soon the lights will come on and the jazz hands will come out. A real gotcha moment. I mean do we really spray toxins on the foods we will eat? Give me ten reasons why we're not a culture of plastic-packaged lemmings? ...Okay, then just one.

Do we really wear turtlenecks?

How funny—us, the butterfingers species, the rebels without a cause. The plainclothes clowns. Like how weird is makeup? Strip clubs? And canned cheese with a squirt nozzle?

Cynicism sure sounds straight right about now. Civilization is practically begging for it. And making fun of it all is way too appealing. But it's also way too easy to stay stuck there. To become part of the joke. To fall in line with folly.

Instead, I stop pretending I know so much. I look around and I open up. And I get back to work. I get back to listening. And I let go of the rest. And I put down my stones.

YOUR ROOTS DEEP

Your leaves beautiful.

But you can't just water

the leaves.

You can't just think truth.

You can't know truth.

You can't know change.

For God's sake, man,

you have to feel it.

You have to live it.

You have to em*body* it.

Now and Then or Whatever

Are we the same, you and I?

Have you plowed through a family's

portion of cookies? Mistakenly massacred

an entire bag of chips? Ice cream, popcorn,

bacon bits, whatever

your vice—have you taken things too far?

Felt shame at the sheer volume

of doughnuts in your belly? Had mixed

feelings of considerable pride yet legitimate

fear at the quantity of jelly beans just

consumed? Well, it's all okay. We all have

a past. I certainly do.

I won't blame you for covertly eating all the chocolate if you don't blame me for all the eggnog I've drank outside the holiday window. It's okay. We'll get through this.

In college, I took a course. Well, not a *course-course*, but I guess an extracurricular course—a week-long breathing course (trust me, the irony is not lost on me, either). Breathing and other things, I guess. We talked a lot (and breathed a lot, sure). Once, the instructor had us close our eyes. She gave us each one grape. She asked us to take our time and eat it, and to simply be aware while doing so.

It seemed silly enough for me to like. So

with eyes still closed, I smiled, and popped

the thing in. A single grape, dark purple

(I guessed). At first I let it sit

in my mouth, this bizarrely smooth,

oblong little thing. I felt its little divet

on the end—where it came from.

It had a belly button, just like me. I found

myself wondering of its journey, this small,

formidable little chap. Who knows its many

adventures? Its many months in a field.

Storm and drought and bug. Then, plucked

from its home. A road trip. A store. A

shopping cart. Now, somehow here. In this

breathing course, or whatever.

85

I bit into it. I almost shouted

it caught me so off-guard as juices

exploded through my mouth,

as its soft flesh transformed, exposing its

delicious, gelatinous guts. This fruit, it was

once alive. Wait, was it still? Was this the

moment of its death? Its decomposition?

Gosh, I'd never really pondered

the estimated time of death

for a fruit before. Is that wrong?

What else have I taken for granted?

Anyways, it made its way around my

mouth, slowly, softly breaking

away and releasing flavors. Gradually,

it gave way to entropy

or creation, not sure which. It must have

been a couple of minutes solid, eating this

fruit. This one grape. By the end I was

smiling. No, I was practically laughing.

How many thousands

of inadequately appreciative bites

have I taken in my life?

If someone ate like this all the time, would

they just freak out and start shooting

rainbows from their palms? Man,

have I really wasted all this

power? Have I forsaken every bite?

And that's when I learned perhaps the

greatest lesson I received in college—or

breathing courses, or whatever. That's when

I learned a certain indifference

about the present. Now there may be

karma, but there is no karma hell-bent

on revenge. The present moment

doesn't come holding a list of complaints.

It has no gavel, no robe, no condescension

in tone. The present moment

is that of a face wearing a question. It asks,

what will you do? No, not someday. Not

deep into the future. But what will you do

with this one moment?

Easy Does It

I'm an odd bird, maybe a bit

ambitious. I have lofty standards for myself

and for our species.

I'm all about getting high

on our highest self, and being peaceful

to our peace of mind. Gratitude is my force

field against unhappiness.

I talk about seeking change,

then work very hard to set about creating it.

Yet, friends and critics still tell me

"it's easier said than done".

But what does saying that *do*?

And what could be done instead of

saying it?

Does it explain or excuse?

Is it declaration or defeatism?

I mean, is it not a self-fulfilling prophecy?

What I'm trying to ask is

does it do *anything*?

Or is it just saying something?

Which, yeah, I guess is easy.

But you know what I say:

what's easier than…done.

Future Oath

I vow to shop for what I believe in

I vow to grow what I can

I vow to know who I support

I vow to not externalize my costs

    but to internalize the consequences

    of my being

    and to be worthy of all the work

    involved in my existence

I vow to not just believe in a future

    but to create it

Monsanto

I won't just give you my good

moments. I won't gloss over my doubts

and fears like the incompleteness

of smiling pictures in a scrapbook,

or the assumed omniscience

of an author.

I stumble lost through the dark

uncertainty, through hope-

lessness. I can't brushstroke away

the depth or scope of our problems.

I can't tell you that it's all going

to be okay, that we're safe.

I can't promise results.

I can only offer you my worldview:

to fulfill one's purpose,

to carry out one's greatest work

here, while not taking oneself

too seriously (such as overusing

the pronoun "oneself").

I give my life,

this moment and every other

one, to changing the world

while at the same time letting

go.

I Am BEAUTIFUL

I am a walking gut pile,

a cringing shriveling mess.

A mish mash of mush and organs,

bloody workhorses, a slop of sweat shop

tactics. Pushing moving rotting fighting

cleaning changing growing.

Parts of me are basically dying,

a cellular kamikaze for the collective.

Parts of me are recooking themselves from

scratch, perfectionist powertripping

sous chefs. Energy packrats. Mucus

pushers. This is my only tangible

grasp at an identity.

These hormonal hooplas, these tunnels

of tubes, these volunteers or slaves,

domestic dungeonites. Goopy grimy do-

gooders never far from a swamp

of acids or bile. A bacterial

boomtown. Pumps and clogs and drains

and valves. Porous ratchety bones

to keep the whole thing afloat.

A scaffolding of calcium. Folded skin,

spongy tissue, rivers of blood.

Consciousness somewhere in the gross

mass of it, which is quite BEAUTIFUL

if you think about it.

Ear Reverent Prayers

We summon strength for we know it is

not easy. What with industrialization,

globalization, and television

dating shows. And all our noise.

We ask for forgiveness for the pollution, for

our wars, and for gummy bears.

Well, not the gummy bears. Sorry.

But to the forces greater than us, may we

hear your music

and play it with our bones

These Days

I know I'm embarking on a dubious

mission: I'm trying to inspire you. But I

won't sweep the drama under the rug.

Often times, I don't know how realistic

hope is. Time will only tell if we've already

tiptoed beyond the event horizon.

But, I'm not sold on that. I take food as a

foundational, direct means to change. And

it is. Or it can be. But the quagmire is that

food can't be isolated—from our

civilization, industrial mindset, or society.

So we can't *just* change our food system, of course. We have to change our system, our whole way of being.

I'm proposing that I believe we can and must start with food. There is no environmentalism on a dirty plate. There is no salvation in a wicked sustenance. But I don't know what will happen. The future draws obscure models. I won't spoonfeed you certainties.

These days, we're running the greatest experiment known to man or woman. We don't know what's to come, because what we're doing has never come before. We are

the guinea pig generations. The ultimate

double blind study. The test subjects are our

hearts, our rivers, our children. Our lungs

and livers and aquifers and seeds. Our

kingdoms, both plant and animal and other.

All subject to our unknowns. Our cocktail of

novelties. Our ocean of new variables.

Ignorance should be the mother of caution.

But we ignore our ignorance, or make it

propaganda. Maybe it's time for the next

greatest experiment: to not hide from

ignorance or distract ourselves from pain,

but to face center to the mirror, with a

vision not a vengeance, and to do whatever

it takes to be worthy of our birth.

What's My Point?

The profound hides in broad daylight,

draped in the camoflauge of the everyday.

Eat the change

you want to see in the world.

At-home-garden and down-the-road-farms.

Agriculture-of-the-sun. Fertilizer-of-the-

waste. Protector-of-the-cycle.

Inheritor-and-giver.

My point is this:

if you think you're powerless

to change things,

you're wrong.

If you think it's all hopeless and

what's the point,

you're missing it.

If you feel that the future is

yet to be decided

by our present,

you just may be on to something.

Now, let's get to it.

Oh, and thanks for listening.

It's been real.

A Healthy Appendix

-Real Ways You Can Help-

Get Dirty – One of the most transformational things you can do is to start growing your own food, becoming in touch with the life-giving forces of the planet. Compost, container garden on a window ledge or patio, make a garden bed, or help someone else on their farm or garden.

Prepare Your Own Grub – When you cook at home, preparing and preserving foods, you remove the harmful processing ingredients, become aware of everything in your food, and take partnership in your sustenance. It's quite powerful and makes positive ripples.

Get Your Learn On – Awareness is the key that unlocks change. This book's resource section alone could keep you busy for a minute. Never stop learning, questioning, and applying.

Eat Your Ethics – As you learn more, or apply what you already know, eat in accordance with your ethics. Make it a priority. It's not a task, as much as it's an honor.

Shop Smart – It doesn't get more effective or concise than Michael Pollan's book *Food Rules*. "Eat real food. Mostly plants. Not too much." I would add that you should support farms directly, go to farmer's markets, co-ops and health food stores, *then* other grocery stores if you must. Buy produce and whole foods; otherwise, read ingredient labels. Beware of marketing. You can shop inexpensively and still support good food. Cut out the junk and soda. Use this money to buy more nutrient-dense vegetables. Buy in bulk, especially better meats.

Vote with Your Food Dollars – This is an important extension of shopping smart. Remember that the choices you make in our economy reflect back to our environment. Spend your dollars in ways that contribute to soil health, biodiversity, protection of our watersheds, and raise the integrity of local farmers. Don't support practices that aren't healthy for us, the environment, the workers, or the animals.

Eat Less Meat – This is our sacred cow (pun very much intended, yes). However, our culture eats way more meat than is necessary. This has huge implications on our bodies, our environment, and of course, on our animal friends. Use meat

as a flavoring agent or a side dish, or go
vegetarian.

Don't Support Factory Farms – If you do eat meat,
there are plenty of healthy, ethical options. If
meat, eggs, milk, etc. is very cheap, those costs
have been transferred elsewhere—to a polluted
environment, to the subsidies of taxpayers, to
our health, or to our ethics.

Raise Awareness – Have conversations, set up
film screenings of important documentaries,
start and sign petitions, organize community
events, infuse your art—whatever art that is—
with awareness.

Get Political – Politics is tricky. You can't be the
easily-dejected type. There are many pains to the
process, but certainly real changes can and must
be made here. Lobbyists, lawyers, protestors,
and politicians with an ecological conscience are
all a necessity today.

Include Your Job – I know this too can get tricky,
but test the waters if your employer is open to
positive changes. In response, they can often get
free positive publicity.

Influence Your School – School lunches are often processed and can be downright unhealthy. Encourage your school or your kids' school to not accept soft drink sponsorship, to get fast food out of there, and to promote more healthy options.

Involve Your University – Colleges and universities are hotbeds for inspired action. Get your peers on board. Shape your cafeterias. Organize your allies. Speak up and speak out.

Eat Sustainable Seafood (and less) – I know fish is good for you, but much of it isn't so healthy anymore. The higher up the food chain, the more toxicity the fish is likely to possess. Since the ocean is out of sight, it is often one of the most harmful and brutal food industries. Investigate your sources. Better yet, catch it yourself, if possible. And treat fish as a special occasion.

Start a Community Garden – If your neighborhood allows for this, get a community garden going. You can often get funding for this through grants or fundraising. This enables the community to come together and get involved with food cultivation.

Support Local and Form Webs – Get to know your farmers, go in on a half-cow with some friends, have meals together, share cooking responsibilities, trade foods from the garden. Build a food web.

Work or Volunteer for Change – FoodCorps is probably the best organization I know of for a work-trade. WWOOF also has volunteering connections to organic farms all around the world. But, it doesn't have to be volunteer work. There are plenty of jobs where you can make a paycheck and a positive impact. Keep your eyes and imagination open.

Donate – If you can't figure out how to help, help someone who's already at it. There are many good organizations putting in serious work. Donations help.

Don't Stop with Food – Food is just the gateway drug. Make your own natural cleaners, work with less toxic materials, use less plastics, tincture up your own medicines, and keep the ripples radiating. Have fun!

Notes for the Poems

I don't think of these as explanations, just alternate expressions, a little more info. I've found that many friends appreciate some extra insight or background into the poems. However, there is always plenty of space for interpretation and many layers I haven't uncovered. So, don't feel like you have to read this or that you should think of the poems in these terms. The poems are now yours. Whatever your experience of the poems, that is their ultimate truth.

<u>Will Work</u> *for Food* [1] - This is where I introduce the premise of the entire book. The first part has many capitalized nouns (The World, The Government, etc.). This is to imply their bigness, their almost unreachable distance from our day-to-day lives. Food, however, is right here. It's small and necessary and right in front of us. And we can transform ourselves through it. "Will Work" and "can" are both underlined to tie these two together. It will work *if* we do. It's our choice.

Dollar Create/shun Dance [2] – The first four couplets give something of a history of commerce, from bartering with your neighbor to the material excesses of today. The pace and style then switch dramatically and challenge us to see ourselves as creators. In a sense this continues the chronology. The making of history in the present. Create/shun = creation. We can build things up. We can let others die down. Oh, and the randomness of the word "laundromat" in the poem, I just thought that was funny. Sorry if you didn't.

Bedtime Stories [4] – This begins a thread throughout the book, the Eastern idea of action with non-attachment to the results. And the Zen of simply experiencing life, rather than staying in our head all the time, telling ourselves these stories (money, wins and losses) that keep us asleep.

For Albert Camus [6] – Inspired by his quote: "Perhaps we cannot prevent this world from being a world in which children are tortured. But we can reduce the number of tortured children." Same thing for the biosphere. Progress not perfection.

(Expertise)-ism [7] – "Know" starts out always underlined, implying the certainty of expert knowledge. "Can" is in parentheses to indicate choice. At the end this switches. "Can" is underlined to give more gravity to the choice of

over-tinkering with nature. "Know" is now in parentheses, to soften their certainty, and to put their knowledge in context of the choices they make.

All foods not created = [10] - This juxtaposes the clean, economic view of the supermarket (in 1 and 2) against the raw, graphic reality of being connected to the life you take (in Three). Though the supermarket looks orderly and pretty, it hides many ugly scenes. Though taking life is difficult and dirty, it has always been considered a sacred necessity. You can't live without death, but there are consequences to outsourcing the killing.

small is Beautiful [13] – This compares the houses of power, politics, with the individual, seen often as a pawn or a victim to forces outside itself. This poem turns that idea upside down. We all see bureaucracy trudging on at a snail's pace (no offense to snails, who have a perfectly suitable pace) and it feels defeating. But our own lives we can change in an instant. And that's not trivial. It starts to radiate out, affecting others, affecting our world.

At the Temple [15] – "THE ECONOMY" is all capitalized in a attempt to convey the type of awe or hysteria given to a god or monster. We often treat our economic activity as something to obey at all costs, forgetting that there's no healthy economy without a healthy world. And that the economy, like all our choices, is part of our creation.

Perfect Food Iz Bad for You [16] – Bad grammar, bad spelling, is it really so bad? If you're Miss Mercer, then yes. Yet, our system demanding perfect appearance of fruits and vegetables leaves countless numbers of them to be thrown away before they ever see a store. We spray them for bugs. We gas them for shelf-life. All in the name of perfection, something every child knows does not exist.

For My Niece Avery (someday) [17] – My niece Avery is one of 3 beautiful girls (each with their own poem). She's still a cute little toddler. This is a "someday" poem for her, when she's becoming her own person and going through the growing pains of evolution. I remind her that this book is for her as much as anyone and that she, too, has the powers of change and the capacity for turning scar tissue into inspiration and blessings.

Compost -the Republic- [19] – When we see ourselves as small and insignificant, it's easy to claim that our actions mean nothing. But when we see ourselves as epic, extraordinary, powerful, we know otherwise. We are not consumers, but producers of the next world. Let's not pass into the sleep of death without being worthy of such a responsibility.

Just a girl [21] – Here the sanitized food of the supermarket is placed against the airbrushed supermodels of the checkout aisle. The first seems a far cry from food in the field. The second seems worlds away from real women. So, in both the food and our women, they have been artificially "perfected", the consequences being taxed to our bodies...and to our self-love.

?uestion Mark at the End [23] – Short poem, but there's still plenty to unpack. Contrary to the title, the question mark is at the very beginning and it ends with a period, standing alone. This is playing with the idea of what I think is either justification or lack of imagination—that our destructive food system is a necessary evil.

Modifying Organisms [24] – This poem uses GMOs to express something even larger—our disconnect from nature-based systems. It's a survive or thrive debate. Will we take in calories or nutrition? Will we take, or will we leave a harmonious and balanced system for our great-grandchildren? The stakes are that high. The ending suggests that maybe the organisms we should be modifying are not other species, but ourselves.

On Cultivating [27] – This poem inserts doubt, even into the validity of this book. Yet it gains momentum in the second stanza with the epiphany that we have no option out of action. Since doing nothing is impossible, doing something is necessary. Might as well be good.

More Like Talking [28] – This is written as prose and has a style more similar to talking than writing, per se—hence the title. It challenges our cherished beliefs on economics, and puts the economy in its necessary—in fact, inescapable—context of ecology. The ending paints a dark image of what will happen if we choose to neglect this natural law. Then, it softens that image, with "…don't worry, we're just talking here." This feels safer, and now the title gains a different meaning: we're more comfortable talking in words and ideas than with on-the-ground, in-the-dirt reality.

113

Out in the Dark (sustenance) [32] – Sometimes its accurate, or at least healthy, to think of the Universe as animate and personal. However, there's also a beauty to indifference, something natural about it, almost honest. Nothing is certain in this life. Perhaps meaning, or sustenance, is somewhere *in* the mystery. Perhaps in the darkness there is a light.

Bhagavad Eata [33] – The title is a play on Bhagavad Gita, the ancient Indian text. That book emphasizes duty or action, without attaching oneself to the results that follow. This poem pokes fun at my own armchair environmentalism, but stresses the notion of living according to your principles without bogging down on the details. It also talks a lot about Diogenes, the ancient Greek philosopher. And bathtubs. Lots of bathtubs.

Enter Net (A World Wide Web) [36] – There's a lot here, but the first stanza shows the pervasiveness of the internet in our lives. It then uses popular rap music of today to illustrate our ego-obsession. Not one love, but one loneliness. Me-ism (mono-typical). I love hip-hop. I write it and study it. But here, I speak out against the money-glorification, violence, and degradation of women, which reflects back to the lesser aspects of our society in general. Then, politics. The stereo-typical. The fighting and the divisiveness. Black and white until we're black and blue, once again reflecting upwards to aspects of our civilization as a whole. To me, the ending encompasses the whole book. Maybe we can start to heal our society and its many problems through the cornerstone of food justice, in every sense of the term.

An Apology (Do You Except?) [40] – Written as if an apology to a lover, this puts together the bizarre and the brutal of what we've done. Ultimately, it asks if the planet will allow us a second chance. Typically, species bust (and not softly) after such a boom as we've had. Yet, if we can relearn to love and respect our biological foundation, is there still time for us?

Attention Deficit [44] – We do seem to have an attention deficit disorder: fear of silence, constant chatter, and isolation in an exclusively human world. This poem uses the wild dandelion (for some reason vilified) to counter that world. We've lost our attention to the non-human beings and systems all around us. Awareness is gratitude.

Don't Have To [50] – There are many things perfectly legal that you probably shouldn't do. There are also many things that no one is forcing you to do—self-realization, compassion, creativity, and making an impact—that are unnecessary, yet provide all the meaning in life. Why not do them? Why not be them?

Teaching Fish to Swim [54] – Fish don't need to be taught to swim. They are born to do so. We, too, were born to survive in this world. We don't need to be re-taught, as much as we need to remember. This is not something I'm placing on myself or others. It's part of the contract of birth.

Supermarket Survivalism [56] – This poem emulates all the background confusion of grocery shopping these days. The pastoral scenes on processed foods. The loaded marketing terms. The superficial diversity of choices. The poem is as confusing as the supermarket (both intentionally so—the poem, to make a point; the supermarket, to make a buck).

"Eating is an agricultural act" [58] – The title is from a quote by Wendell Berry. It applies it further to the point that agriculture occurs in the

realm of the biosphere — our air, soil, and water. We pollute all of these, much of which with our food industries. But this also means we can start to remedy many of these problems by cleaning up our plate.

Poor People [61] – Partly I had in mind a popular internet joke that my sister sent me years ago, of St. Francis explaining the American lawn to God. But I wanted to give some more layers to that general idea by adding a naïve narrator. This amps up the ridiculousness, but also provides a different standard for normal. The ending foreshadows our present, where our lawn-obsession (and monocultures in general) are completely seen as normal. Pobrecitos.

The Paradox of THE WORLD [69] – This again confronts the confusion of choice, once again in the context of just trying to have a decent meal. The double-commas, to me, symbolize the excesses that today cloud what was once quite simple. This happens to the point of consequence, whether we mistakenly eat unhealthy food, or like the ending, miss breakfast altogether. Dang it.

Smells Fishy [73] – This poem is pretty straightforward. It challenges our ocean-sized euphemisms. Whether long-lining, bottom trawling, or the many other mega-contraptions cooked up by industrial fleets, to call this "fishing" must be a misnomer. My apologies to the Buddhists for bringing up their spiritual leader. I understand they're a very ill-tempered people that get easily riled up about their dogmatic religion.

Looking Glass, Houses and Stones [77] – In this poem, I'm wrestling with my cynical side, something that makes a great deal of sense at times. Though however realistic cynicism may be, it has drawbacks. It closes you off to alternative explanations, and opens you up to apathy. But it's still kind of fun.

YOUR ROOTS DEEP [81] – I put the title in all-caps as a nod to David Byrne (of Talking Heads) and his "big suit". He wore that suit at times to convey the idea that we feel and experience music in our bodies much sooner than we intellectually understand it. I think it's the same thing with whatever that truth stuff is.

Now and Then or Whatever [83] – Many Buddhist monks chew their food 30 or 40 times each bite. What a difference mindful eating provides. This recounts an experience I had during a course with The Art of Living. For me, it reminds us that the present moment allows for re-creation…instantly. And that grapes are good. Really, really good.

Easy Does It [89] – I've heard this comment so many times I find myself reaching for a therapist's sofa. "Easier said than done". While I understand its source, I'm no fan of this statement. In my book (which this is…laugh out loud, emoticon), I think its easier than what we give ourselves credit for with such self-defeating rhetoric.

Future Oath [91] – The title is a subtle play on words. It's an oath that I hope more and more of us are making in the future. But, it's also an oath for the future, to make it even possible.

Monsanto [92] – If you know anything of the agribusiness corporation or the controversy surrounding them, you might anticipate the poem going differently based on the title. I wanted to include the context of big problems and big powers without doing it the same old way. I wanted to take the fear and doubt we feel with the political process or with large-scale, multinational corporations and transform it into a teaching. To take our weaknesses and vulnerabilities as opportunities for evolution.

I Am BEAUTIFUL [94] – I'm a sucker for comedy. I take the Zen-like stance that absurdity is close enough to enlightenment. Yet, there are some meat and potatoes here to all this gut talk…(pun not intended…no, wait, intended…ah, forget it). We often forget all the tiny forces within us that make life even possible. A lot of this stuff is, well, gross. But, even supermodels have guts and bile. And as any elementary reader has already learned, everybody poops. I think we get stuck on the icky factor; but all that transpires from digestion to consciousness and beyond is also awe-inspiring and beautiful. So, it's a little sloppy. So what?

Ear Reverent Prayers [96] – This poem is a defiant manifesto justifying the existence of gummy bears.

These Days [97] – This one is definitely more prosaic and, for me, marks the beginning of the conclusion. We were not born into a neat and simple world. The challenges we face are great. Yet, we must face them. To run and hide is a type of death.

What's My Point? [101] – [The reader thinks: "Finally…"] This is it: my big conclusion, my grand finale…"'It's been real'?...Wait...It's been real? Are you serious? Who finishes a book like that?" Hey, I'm working on it, okay.

Suggested Media

-Suggested Documentaries/Films-

Some of these can be found for free on popular media sites such as YouTube, Netflix, and others. Even watching the trailers for free online would be a worthwhile experience.

Fresh (2009) – This documentary is very upbeat and encouraging, highlighting innovative farmers and food growers serving as real-life examples of change. It's a great one to show family members or those new to the issues.

Food, Inc. (2008) – Upon release, this well-produced classic opened many eyes to the ugly realities of industrial food production — for us, the animals, and the planet. Further, it emphasizes the importance of how we each vote with our food dollars. Every time we eat or buy food, we are voting for who and what we support.

Fed Up (2014) – Katie Couric takes us to heart of the childhood obesity epidemic, and its reaches into adulthood. It examines the primary role that added sugars and processed foods have had in contributing to our national health crisis, and how private profit has been put before public health.

Dirt! The Movie (2009) – Explores the world beneath our feet, and the precious layer of topsoil that our lives literally depend on. This film reminds us that dirt is not just precious, it's worth more than gold.

Cowspiracy (2014) – This documentary focuses in on one of the world's most harmful industries, animal agriculture, and talks about…why nobody's talking about it. The film presses heavy on our system of raising cattle, and its sustainability considering the enormous demands on water and land, and the resulting pollution.

King Corn (2007) – A fun ride and a serious look at the monolithic position of corn in our food system. This film explains how government subsidies of corn artificially rig the game, and then what happens with our surplus of this product—primarily finding its way into our processed foods and onto our waists.

Food Chains (2014) – Reveals the human cost of our food and what can be done to restore integrity to our farm workers. An empowering, seldom-heard story.

Dive! Living off America's Waste (2009) – Gourmet-eating dumpster divers that would make Thoreau proud? Absolutely. Examines how much food we waste (a lot!), why it happens, and how it can change.

A Place at the Table (2012) – From the same folks who made Food, Inc., this is an in-depth look into the suprising amount of hunger and food insecurity in the United States.

Symphony of the Soil (2013) – A beautiful and fascinating glimpse into how miraculous our precious soil is, and why it's so vital to protect it.

Some others to check out: *Food Fight* (2008) *Bite Size* (2014), *Just Eat It: a food waste story* (2014), *Forks over Knives* (2011), *The Future of Food* (2004),

The Garden (2008), *Vegucated* (2011), *Hungry for Change* (2012)

-Suggested Internet Resources-

Websites change. Sorry about that. However, I thought it was still worthwhile to give some resources for the web.

http://www.ampleharvest.org/

   - connects food growers to food pantries

http://www.animalwelfareapproved.org/

   - look for their label on meat, dairy, and eggs

http://www.beyondpesticides.org/

   - great info on pesticides and moving beyond them

http://www.certifiedhumane.org/

   - label for meat, dairy, eggs, and poultry

http://www.civileats.com/

   - daily news about the food system

http://www.ciw-online.org/

- learn more on farm workers' issues

http://www.deconstructingdinner.com/

- simplifies food choices and information

http://www.eatwellguide.org/

- find local food restaurants, farms, and markets

http://www.eatwild.com/

- find healthy, local meats, dairy, and eggs

http://www.ewg.org/

- great consumer info on food/healthy products

https://www.farmersmarketcoalition.org/

- resources/info for farmers and customers

http://www.factoryfarmmap.org/

- both a fascinating and terrifying map

http://www.farmtoschool.org/

- local food in schools, school gardens, education

https://www.foodcorps.org/

- service work/Americorps for the food movement

http://www.frugalmamafiles.com/2013/07/meal-planning-how-we-live-on-75-week.html

 - *some tips on budgeting for good food in the home*

http://www.grist.org/food/

 - *stories and news from the food frontier*

http://www.localharvest.org/

 - *find farms and markets near you*

http://www.michaelpollan.com/resources/

 - *plenty more amazing resources*

http://www.motherearthnews.com/

 - *still one of the best resources for natural living*

http://www.nrdc.org/oceans/seafoodguide/

 - *how to eat fish sustainably and ethically*

http://www.realfoodchallenge.org/

 - *unites students for just and sustainable food*

http://www.sustainabletable.org/

 - *comprehensive resources on eating sustainably*

http://www.usdalocalfooddirectories.com/listings.html

   - find farmers markets and CSA's

http://www.whatsonmyfood.org/

   - learn about the pesticides on different foods

https://www.wholesomewave.org/

   - making sustainable food affordable

http://www.wildfermentation.com/

   - learn to preserve foods and boost their nutrients

http://www.wwoof.net/

   - World Wide Opportunities on Organc Farms

-Suggested Reading-

Good ol' books. Still can't beat 'em. Tap into your library for a free peak, and support your local bookstores.

Barber, Dan. *The Third Plate: Field Notes on the Future of Food*. Penguin Press, 2014.

Berry, Wendell. *Bringing it to the Table: On Farming and Food*. Counterpoint, 2009

Berry, Wendell. *New Collected Poems*. Counterpoint, 2012.

Berry, Wendell. *The Art of the Commonplace: The Agrarian Essays*. Counterpoint, 2002.

Berry, Wendell. *The Gift of Good Land: Further Essays Cultural and Agricultural*. North Point Press, 1981.

Berry, Wendell. *The Unsettling of America: Cutlure and Agriculture*. Counterpoint, 1977.

Berthold-Bond, Annie. *Better Basics for the Home: Simple Solutions for Less Toxic Living*. Three Rivers Press, 1999.

Brown, Leanne. *Good and Cheap: Eat Well on $4/Day*. Workman Publishing Company, 2014.

Falk, Ben. *The Resilient Farm and Homestead: An Innovative Permaculture and Whole Systems Design Approach.* Chelsea Green Publishing, 2013.

Hanh, Thich Nhat. *Love Letter to the Earth.* Parallax Press, 2013.

Hanh, Thich Nhat and Lilian Cheung. *Savor: Mindful Eating, Mindful Life.* HarperOne, 2011.

Hartwig, Dallas and Melissa. *It Starts with Food: Discover the Whole30 and Change Your Life in Unexpected Ways.* Victory Belt Publishing, 2012.

Kingsolver, Barbara. *Animal, Vegetable, Miracle: A Year of Food Life.* HarperCollins, 2007.

Lappé, Frances Moore. *EcoMind: Changing the Way We Think, to Create the World We Want.* Nation Books, 2011.

Leake, Lisa. *100 Days of Real Food: How We Did It, What We Learned, and 100 Easy, Wholesome Recipes Your Family Will Love.* William Morrow Cookbooks, 2014.

Macy, Joanna and Chris Johnstone. *Active Hope: How to Face the Mess We're in without Going Crazy.* New World Library, 2012.

Madigan, Carleen. *The Backyard Homestead: Produce all the food you need on just a quarter acre.* Storey Publishing, 2009.

Mollison, Bill. *Permaculture: A Designer's Manual.* Tagari Publications, 1988.

Nestle, Marion. *Food Politics*. University of California Press, 2002.

Nestle, Marion. *What to Eat*. North Point Press, 2006.

Oliver, Mary. *New and Selected Poems*. Beacon Press, 1992.

Oliver, Mary. *New and Selected Poems: Volume 2*. Beacon Press, 2007.

Pollan, Michael. *Cooked: A Natural History of Transformation*. Penguin Press, 2013.

Pollan, Michael. *Food Rules: An Eater's Manual*. Penguin Press, 2009.

Pollan, Michael. *In Defense of Food: An Eater's Manifesto*. Penguin Press, 2008

Pollan, Michael. *The Omnivore's Dilemma: A Natural History of Four Meals*. Penguin Press, 2006.

Robinson, Jo. *Eating on the Wild Side: The Missing Link to Optimal Health*. Little, Brown and Company, 2013.

Salatin, Joel. *Folks, This Ain't Normal: A Farmer's Advice for Happier Hens, Healthier People, and a Better World*. Center Street, 2011.

Schlosser, Eric. *Fast Food Nation: The Dark Side of the All-American Meal*. Houghton Mifflin, 2001.

Singer, Peter and Jim Mason. *The Ethics of What We Eat: Why Our Food Choices Matter*. Rodale Books, 2007.

Solomon, Steve and Erica Reinheimer. *The Intelligent Gardener: Growing Nutrient-Dense Food*. New Society Publishers, 2013.

-Suggested Magazines-

Acres USA. Acres USA Publishing.

Mother Earth News. Ogden Publications.

Orion. The Orion Society.

Thanks so much for spending some time with me. I hope it's been a blessing for both of us. Feel free to reach out to me at jposeyone@gmail.com. One as in love.

Please check me out on Etsy and Amazon. I'm small-time, so leaving a review would be deeply appreciated. Keep an eye out for other projects of our family, Sacred Task.

A special thanks to the trees for their sacrifice. It's my hope that the words of this book may honor their lives and that we can regrow them in ourselves and in our world.

Lastly, I hope when you put this book down from your hands, you keep it in your heart. I believe in you. I believe in us.

-jp

Made in the USA
San Bernardino, CA
25 April 2016